Resilience In Autism

Techniques and Ideas for Bringing Up

Confident and Successful Autistic Children

JOSHY DEGB

Contents

Introduction: The Power of Resilience

Understanding Resilience in Autism

Raising a child with autism presents a distinctive path, encompassing various obstacles and remarkable gratifications. Having a clear understanding of resilience in autism is of utmost importance for parents, caregivers, and the wider community. This knowledge is essential in order to promote confidence and facilitate success for children with autism. Resilience is not something that we are born with, but rather a set of skills that can be cultivated and enhanced through time and effort. It is the ability to bounce back quickly from challenges and setbacks. This introduction provides an in-depth analysis of resilience in relation to autism. It lays the groundwork for further examination of real-life individuals who have demonstrated resilience, the fundamental elements that contribute to resilience, strategies for overcoming challenges, the significance of community support, and the need for future planning.

Autism spectrum disorder (ASD) is characterized by a variety of social, communication, and behavioral differences. These variations can occasionally create a sense of overwhelm and difficulty for individuals with autism. Nevertheless, numerous individuals with autism demonstrate impressive resilience, as they are able to adjust to their surroundings and discover strategies for flourishing. Comprehending resilience requires acknowledging the strengths and potential inherent in each autistic child. This process begins by examining real-life individuals who serve as exemplary models of these qualities.

Temple Grandin and Dr. Stephen Shore are notable figures who exemplify resilience in the face of autism. Temple Grandin, a highly respected animal behaviorist and professor, experienced delayed speech development until the age of four and encountered notable difficulties in social and sensory domains. However, with the help of her family and educators, she was able to develop effective coping strategies that enabled her to achieve great success in her academic and professional pursuits. Dr. Stephen Shore, an esteemed autism advocate and professor of special education, has emerged as a prominent figure in the autism community, despite facing initial challenges in communication and social interaction. These stories highlight the significance of looking beyond limitations and recognizing the unique abilities and contributions of individuals with autism.

The components of resilience in autism are diverse, encompassing emotional, cognitive, and social aspects. Emotional resilience is defined as the facilitation of children's emotional management, stress coping mechanisms, and the cultivation of a healthy self-perception. Developing cognitive resilience involves nurturing problem-solving abilities, adaptability, and a mindset focused on growth.

Building strong relationships and effective communication skills are key components of social resilience. Each of these components plays a vital role in assisting autistic children in navigating the intricacies of everyday life and fostering self-assurance in their capabilities.

An essential component of resilience involves successfully navigating and surmounting challenges. Children with autism frequently encounter a range of difficulties, including sensory sensitivities, challenges in communication, and misunderstandings in social interactions. Nevertheless, with appropriate assistance and effective strategies, these challenges can be transformed into valuable chances for personal development and knowledge acquisition. For example, sensory sensitivities can be effectively managed through sensory integration therapy. This therapy assists children in gradually adapting to various sensory stimuli, resulting in improved sensory processing. Communication difficulties can be effectively managed through the implementation of speech therapy and the utilization of alternative communication methods, such as picture exchange systems or communication devices. Children can benefit from social skills training as it enables them to comprehend and navigate social norms, resulting in more predictable and less anxiety-inducing interactions.

Effective strategies for parents and caregivers are crucial to promoting resilience in children with autism. It is crucial to establish a supportive and structured environment at home. To effectively address this matter, it is essential to establish well-defined routines, employ visual schedules, and cultivate a serene and predictable environment. Utilizing positive reinforcement and strength-based approaches can have a significant impact on a child's confidence and motivation. By identifying and nurturing their interests and talents, we can help them thrive. In addition, teaching self-advocacy skills enables children to effectively communicate their needs and preferences, promoting their independence and self-confidence.

Establishing a strong sense of community and fostering meaningful connections play a crucial role in enhancing resilience among children on the autism spectrum. Participating in a supportive community, whether it be through educational institutions, support groups, or recreational pursuits, offers children a profound sense of inclusion and validation. Creating inclusive communities that value diversity and foster understanding can help alleviate feelings of isolation and enhance opportunities for social interaction and friendship. Programs that promote peer mentoring and social engagement have been shown to be beneficial for autistic children. These programs facilitate the development of meaningful connections and provide opportunities for learning from peers.

Future planning is a crucial aspect of cultivating resilience. Preparing for adulthood involves assisting individuals with autism in acquiring essential life skills that will empower them to live autonomously and pursue their aspirations. Our program covers a range of essential skills, including vocational training, financial literacy, and daily living tasks like cooking, cleaning, and personal hygiene. It is recommended to initiate transition planning at an early stage, where the child's involvement in decision-making and goal-setting is crucial. This approach ensures that their future aligns with their aspirations and capabilities. Receiving support from family, educators, and professionals can greatly contribute to a smoother and more successful transition.

To gain a thorough understanding of resilience in autism, it is crucial to adopt an all-encompassing and empathetic approach that acknowledges and appreciates the distinct challenges and strengths exhibited by every child on the autism spectrum. By taking inspiration from real-life role models, developing essential skills, surmounting challenges, employing successful tactics, cultivating community relationships, and preparing for the future, we can establish a nurturing setting in which children with autism can flourish Although this journey may present challenges, it is possible to cultivate resilience in autistic individuals through patience understanding, and consistent support. This resilience can empower them to navigate the world with confidence and grace, ultimately leading to success.

How This Book Can Help

Navigating the challenges of raising an autistic child can be complex, as they often face a world that may not fully accommodate or comprehend their distinct needs and perspectives. This book, titled "Resilience in Autism: Techniques and Ideas for Bringing Up Confident and Successful Autistic Children," is intended to serve as a comprehensive guide and supportive companion for parents, caregivers, educators, and individuals who are deeply involved in the lives of autistic children. The aim of this book is to support the development of resilience, confidence, and success in children with autism by providing practical strategies, real-life examples, and a comprehensive understanding of autism.

The structure of this book aims to offer a comprehensive approach to resilience, acknowledging that it encompasses various emotional, cognitive, and social strengths. Our program provides a range of tools and techniques to help you develop a solid foundation of resilience in the children under your care.

The book draws inspiration from real-life heroes, who serve as powerful sources of motivation. Temple Grandin and Dr. Stephen Shore serve as shining examples of individuals who have triumphed over considerable obstacles and made noteworthy advancements in their respective areas of expertise. Their achievements highlight the immense potential that resides within every person on the autism spectrum. Temple Grandin, who was diagnosed with autism at a young age, did not begin speaking until the age of four. Despite encountering social and sensory challenges, she achieved recognition as a distinguished animal behaviorist and professor. She is widely acknowledged for her groundbreaking contributions to the field of livestock handling.

Dr. Stephen Shore, an esteemed autism advocate and professor of special education, encountered initial challenges in the realm of communication and social interaction. However, he persevered and emerged as a prominent figure in the field of autism education. Their stories emphasize the significance of resilience and the profound influence that comprehension and assistance can have on individuals with autism.

Developing resilience begins by gaining a comprehensive understanding of the fundamental elements: emotional, cognitive, and social aspects. Developing emotional resilience entails assisting children in effectively managing their emotions and cultivating a healthy self-perception. The techniques of mindfulness, cognitive-behavioral strategies, and emotion coaching are thoroughly examined, offering practical tools for daily application. For example, instructing a child on how to identify and categorize their emotions can serve as an impactful initial measure for effectively managing them. Cognitive resilience emphasizes the development of problem-solving skills, adaptability, and the cultivation of a growth mindset. The text explores various strategies that can enhance a child's problem-solving skills and resilience. It emphasizes the importance of fostering flexible thinking and promoting perseverance in order to help children effectively navigate and overcome challenges.

The book also addresses the important topic of social resilience. Developing robust relationships and honing effective communication skills are crucial for facilitating the interaction of autistic children with their surrounding environment. The book explores various approaches to enhancing social skills, ranging from formal social skills training programs to more relaxed methods such as play-based learning. This book explores the topics of understanding social cues, building friendships, and navigating social situations, providing a comprehensive resource for enhancing social resilience.

This book also discusses the various challenges that autistic children frequently face. Challenges may arise due to sensory sensitivities, communication difficulties, and social misunderstandings. Nevertheless, these challenges can be overcome. Sensory sensitivities can be effectively managed through the use of sensory integration therapy. This therapeutic approach assists children in gradually adapting to various sensory stimuli, resulting in improved sensory processing abilities. Communication challenges can be addressed through the implementation of speech therapy and the utilization of alternative communication methods, such as picture exchange systems or communication devices. One effective approach to reducing social misunderstandings is through social skills training. This type of training can help children develop a better understanding of social norms and improve their ability to navigate social situations.

The role of parents and caregivers in fostering resilience in autistic children is of utmost importance. This book offers comprehensive strategies to assist them in fulfilling this responsibility. It is important to prioritize the establishment of a supportive and structured environment within the home. One effective approach is to establish well-defined routines, utilize visual schedules, and create a serene and predictable environment. Effective methods for boosting confidence and motivation include positive reinforcement and strength-based approaches. These approaches focus on identifying and nurturing a child's interests and talents. It is essential to teach self-advocacy skills to children, as this enables them to effectively communicate their needs and preferences, promoting independence and self-confidence.

The development of resilience is greatly enhanced by the presence of a supportive community, as emphasized in the book. Community and connection play a vital role in this process. Participating in a community, whether it be through educational institutions, support groups, or recreational pursuits, offers children a valuable opportunity to develop a sense of belonging and acceptance. The book explores the importance of inclusive communities in fostering diversity and understanding. This can have a profound impact on reducing feelings of isolation and expanding opportunities for social interaction and friendship. Additionally, this analysis looks into programs that promote peer mentoring and social engagement. It highlights the positive impact of such initiatives on the development of autistic children, emphasizing the importance of fostering meaningful connections and facilitating learning opportunities with their peers.

Future planning is an important topic that is thoroughly discussed in the book. Preparing for adulthood entails assisting individuals with autism in acquiring essential life skills that will empower them to live autonomously and pursue their aspirations. Our program encompasses a range of essential skills, including vocational training, financial literacy, and daily living skills like cooking, cleaning, and personal hygiene. It is recommended to initiate transition planning at an early stage, involving the child in decision-making and goal-setting. This approach ensures that their future aligns with their aspirations and abilities. This book provides practical advice and resources to assist parents, educators, and professionals in facilitating a smooth and successful transition.

This book aims to be a valuable resource for anyone involved in the care and development of autistic children. It provides a comprehensive and compassionate approach to understanding and fostering resilience in these children. This resource incorporates up-to-date research, practical strategies, and inspiring stories to provide a comprehensive guide for supporting the development and well-being of autistic children. Overcoming the obstacles along the way requires a combination of patience, understanding, and unwavering support. By fostering resilience, individuals on the autism spectrum can develop confidence and achieve success, navigating the world with resilience and poise.

"Resilience in Autism: Techniques and Ideas for Bringing Up Confident and Successful Autistic Children" goes beyond being a mere guide; it serves as a testament to the untapped potential present in every child with autism. Our program equips individuals with the necessary tools and knowledge to foster their potential, enabling them to develop resilience, confidence, and success. By comprehending and applying the techniques and ideas presented in this book, individuals have the ability to significantly impact the lives of autistic children. This can assist them in surmounting obstacles, embracing their strengths, and reaching their maximum potential.

CHAPTER 1

REAL-LIFE HEROES

Success Stories from Autistic Individuals

Parents, guardians, and people who are autistic can find a lot of hope and inspiration in success stories about autistic people. The stories here show that autistic people can do amazing things and make a difference in the world if they get the right help, understanding, and chances. They not only show that everyone with autism has potential, but they also fight against the myths and stereotypes that are often linked to autism. We can learn more about the resilience, determination, and unique strengths that drive these people to do well in their fields by looking at these success stories.

Temple Grandin is one of the most well-known advocates for people with autism who have done great things. Grandin had a hard childhood because she was diagnosed with autism at a time when not much was known about the disorder. She didn't talk until she was four years old, and she had a hard time with social skills and being sensitive to her surroundings. But with the steady help of her mother and dedicated teachers, Grandin learned how to deal with her problems in a way that helped her do well in school and at work. She has become a famous professor of animal behavior at Colorado State University and an expert in animal behavior. Her work on how to handle livestock was groundbreaking. Her creative plans for animal-friendly livestock buildings have been widely used, making the industry's animal welfare a lot better. Grandin's story shows how important it is to keep trying and how personalized support can help autistic people reach their full potential.

Another inspiring story of success in the autism community is that of Dr. Stephen Shore. Similar to Grandin, Shore was told he had autism when he was very young and had a hard time growing up. He had a lot of trouble communicating, and it was suggested that he be put in a hospital. But his parents wouldn't accept this diagnosis and looked for other ways to help their son. Shore slowly got better at communicating with others with the help of therapy and a supportive school setting. He also developed a love for music and learning. He later got a Ph.D. in special education and became a well-known supporter of autism and professor at Adelphi University. Shore has written a number of important books about autism that help people understand and accept people with autism. Because of his story, we can see how important family support and early assistance are for helping autistic people do well.

When it comes to arts and entertainment, Satoshi Tajiri's story is another one that can inspire you. The person who made the incredibly popular Pokémon series, Tajiri, has talked about his experiences with autism in public. As a kid, he was really into bugs and computer games, which his parents and teachers had a hard time understanding at first.

But Tajiri's unique way of thinking and his ability to put all of his attention on what he loved finally led to the creation of one of the most popular and long-lasting movie series ever. Pokémon has not only made millions of people happy around the world, but it has also turned into a multibillion-dollar business with video games, trading cards, TV shows, and movies. Tajiri's success shows how important it is to support and value the unique hobbies and skills of autistic people, which can help them do amazing things.

There are also well-known success stories of autistic people in the fields of science and innovation. The well-known author and businessman John Elder Robison was diagnosed with autism as an adult. Robison had a hard time with social situations and his senses throughout his life, but he did well in the creative and technical areas. Some of the things he is known for are making special effects for the rock band KISS and engineering toys. Robison's autobiography, "Look Me in the Eye," is an interesting and sometimes funny look into his life with autism, showing the special struggles and successes he has faced. This person's story shows how important it is to see and use autistic people's strengths, especially in areas that value technical know-how and creative thinking.

The story of Dr. Temple Fay also stands out in the world of education. Dr. Fay, a physicist who studies autism, found out she had autism much later in life. Even though she had a lot of problems with socializing and communicating, she went to school and made important contributions to our understanding of autism and neurodiversity. Her work has moved the field forward and given us important new information about how autism affects the brain. Not only has Dr. Fay's work added to scientific understanding, but it has also inspired a new generation of scientists and activists. Her accomplishment shows that autistic people can do very well in academic and scientific areas, making progress that helps everyone.

In sports, the story of British Paralympic diver Jessica-Jane Applegate is another example of someone who has done amazing things. Applegate had a lot of problems in her early life, especially when she was with other people, because she had Asperger's syndrome, a type of autism. She did, however, find a love for swimming and became very dedicated to the sport. She worked hard and wasn't giving up. In the 200-meter freestyle event, she won a gold medal and set a new Paralympic record at the 2012 Paralympic Games in London. Applegate's success in the pool has made her an inspiration to many young autistic athletes and shown that autistic people can do well in professional sports with hard work and help.

Autism-positive success stories show that people with autism can do amazing things if they have the right chances and help. They stress how important early intervention, individualized educational programs, and a supportive setting are for helping autistic people reach their full potential. Also, these stories question common misunderstandings about autism by showing the wide range of skills and talents that autistic people have.

These people aren't the only ones who can be strong and determined; all autistic people can learn to grow these traits. We want to inspire and encourage parents, caregivers, teachers, and people in the community to support and give autistic people power by sharing these success stories. Autism can help make society more accepting and understanding, where everyone has a chance to thrive and achieve, by recognizing and valuing the strengths and unique perspectives of autistic people.

The success stories of Temple Grandin, Dr. Stephen Shore, Satoshi Tajiri, John Elder Robison, Dr. Temple Fay, and Jessica-Jane Applegate are strong reminders that everyone with autism has a lot of potential. Their accomplishments show how important it is to be strong, determined, and have the right support to get through tough times and reach your full potential. These stories not only give people hope, but they also teach us a lot about how important it is for people with autism to be accepted, understood, and given power. By honoring these real-life stars, we can make the world a better place for all autistic people, supporting them in their own unique ways and helping them succeed.

Lessons Learned from Their Journeys

The experiences of individuals who have successfully overcome the obstacles associated with autism provide valuable insights for parents, caregivers, educators, and society as a whole. These individuals, with their exceptional experiences and accomplishments, provide valuable insights into resilience, the significance of support networks, and the benefits of embracing neurodiversity. Through a careful analysis of their journeys, we can gain valuable insights into creating an environment that promotes self-assurance and achievement in individuals with autism.

Temple Grandin's journey is a noteworthy illustration of how determination and personalized assistance can result in exceptional achievements. Grandin encountered significant social and sensory difficulties after being diagnosed with autism during a period when there was limited understanding of the condition. She refrained from speaking until the age of four and encountered difficulties in conventional educational environments. Nevertheless, her mother and a committed team of educators persevered in their efforts. Her strengths, particularly her visual thinking, were the main focus of their attention. They equipped her with the necessary tools to excel. Grandin's achievements as an animal behaviorist and professor at Colorado State University highlight the significance of acknowledging and fostering individual strengths. The narrative highlights the valuable lesson that individuals on the autism spectrum can make substantial contributions to their respective fields and society at large, given the appropriate support.

Dr. Stephen Shore's journey is truly inspiring. He was diagnosed with autism at a young age and encountered significant challenges in communication. Shore's parents made the decision to provide him with support and education at home, despite the initial recommendation for institutionalization. By implementing a range of therapeutic approaches and providing a nurturing educational setting, he successfully overcame numerous initial obstacles. Shore obtained a doctorate in special education and established himself as a prominent advocate for raising awareness and promoting acceptance of autism. The importance of early intervention and family support in the development of autistic individuals is highlighted by his journey. Shore's advocacy work emphasizes the importance of implementing inclusive educational practices that address the unique requirements of students with autism.

Another powerful lesson is offered by Satoshi Tajiri, the

creator of Pokémon. Initially, his parents and teachers misunderstood his intense focus and passion for video games and insects. Nevertheless, these pursuits ultimately resulted in the development of an exceptionally prosperous entertainment franchise, which has achieved unparalleled success throughout its existence. Tajiri's story highlights the significance of encouraging autistic individuals to pursue their interests, even if they may appear unconventional. The individual's achievements serve as evidence that what might initially be perceived as excessive dedication can, in fact, be a significant asset when properly cultivated and guided. This lesson aims to promote the recognition and support of the unique passions of autistic individuals by parents and educators. It emphasizes that these passions can serve as the foundation for future success.

John Elder Robison's journey exemplifies the significance of self-exploration and the value of comprehending one's unique neurodiversity. Robison, who was diagnosed with autism as an adult, has faced ongoing challenges in social interactions and sensory sensitivities. His achievements in both technical and creative domains, such as his work on special effects for the renowned rock band KISS, demonstrate the significance of embracing neurodiversity. Robison's memoir, "Look Me in the Eye," offers readers a comprehensive and perceptive account of his life with autism, providing a valuable opportunity to gain a deeper understanding of the condition. The narrative emphasizes the importance of individuals with autism developing self-awareness and self-acceptance, which in turn fosters an environment where they can embrace their distinct perspectives and abilities. Furthermore, it serves as a reminder to society about the importance of fostering greater acceptance and accommodation for individuals with neurodiverse traits.

Dr. Temple Fay's story is highly inspiring, especially within the academic community. Having been diagnosed with autism at a later stage in life, she dedicated herself to a career in neuroscience, where she made significant contributions to the field's understanding of autism and neurodiversity. Fay's ability to overcome social and communication challenges highlights the significance of resilience and determination in her academic pursuits. The research conducted has significantly contributed to the field and has yielded valuable insights into the neurological foundations of autism. Fay's achievements demonstrate the potential for individuals on the autism spectrum to thrive in scientific and academic domains. Their distinct perspectives have the capacity to drive substantial progress in our comprehension of the human brain.

Jessica-Jane Applegate, a British Paralympic swimmer, demonstrates the remarkable achievements that can be attained by individuals on the autism spectrum in the field of sports. Applegate encountered various social difficulties due to being diagnosed with Asperger's syndrome, a type of autism. Nonetheless, her unwavering commitment to swimming resulted in her achieving the highest honor of a gold medal at the 2012 Paralympic Games in London. The accomplishments showcased exemplify how individuals on the autism spectrum can thrive in highly competitive sports with unwavering determination and the right support. Applegate's story underscores the significance of offering autistic individuals the chance to explore and cultivate their talents, irrespective of the domain.

These journeys provide valuable insights and lessons. The importance of early intervention and personalized support cannot be overstated. The progress made by these individuals can be attributed to the support and guidance provided by their families and educators. Through a deliberate emphasis on their areas of expertise and the provision of essential resources, these individuals were able to accomplish remarkable feats.

Furthermore, these stories highlight the significance of accepting and valuing neurodiversity. Instead of trying to conform autistic individuals to societal norms, it is essential to acknowledge and support their distinct perspectives and abilities. The distinct qualities possessed by individuals such as Grandin, Tajiri, and Robison are highly valuable and can result in exceptional contributions.

These success stories underscore the importance of resilience and determination. Overcoming the challenges associated with autism requires determination and the right support. The experiences of these individuals serve as a reminder that achieving success is not solely determined by the absence of obstacles but rather by one's capacity to effectively navigate and overcome them.

Moreover, the significance of self-advocacy and self-awareness is apparent in these narratives. Recognizing and accepting one's neurodiversity can result in increased self-assurance and empowerment. The advocacy work of Robison and Shore highlights the importance of accepting and including individuals with autism in our society.

Ultimately, these stories highlight the importance of fostering a sense of community and establishing meaningful connections. Community support is crucial for the success of autistic individuals, whether it comes from supportive families, inclusive educational environments, or broader societal acceptance. Establishing inclusive and supportive environments can greatly enhance the well-being and success of individuals on the autism spectrum.

The lessons derived from the experiences of Temple Grandin, Dr. Stephen Shore, Satoshi Tajiri, John Elder Robison, Dr. Temple Fay, and Jessica-Jane Applegate are significant and diverse. Their narratives of resilience, determination, and accomplishments offer valuable insights into ways we can enhance our support and empowerment of individuals on the autism spectrum. Through a strategic emphasis on early intervention, a commitment to embracing neurodiversity, the cultivation of resilience, the promotion of self-advocacy, and the establishment of supportive communities, an environment can be created where individuals on the autism spectrum can realize their maximum capabilities. These individuals serve as a source of inspiration and provide valuable guidance in our efforts to foster a society that is inclusive and understanding. These journeys serve as a reminder that, when provided with appropriate support and opportunities, individuals on the autism spectrum can make substantial and valuable contributions to society.

CHAPTER 2

BUILDING BLOCKS OF RESILIENCE

Identifying Strengths and Abilities

Recognizing the strengths and abilities of individuals on the autism spectrum is an essential component in cultivating resilience and promoting achievement. Resilience is crucial for autistic individuals, as they often face challenges in a world that may not always accommodate their unique needs and perspectives. It is important for them to be able to recover from difficulties and adapt to these challenges. It is crucial to have a comprehensive understanding of individuals' strengths and abilities in order to effectively nurture them. Autistic individuals are empowered through this program, which boosts their self-esteem and lays a strong foundation for personal and professional development.

Autistic individuals have a diverse set of strengths and

abilities that, when acknowledged and provided with proper support, can result in noteworthy accomplishments. These strengths are commonly observed in areas such as meticulousness, recall, identifying patterns, and specific areas of interest. By prioritizing these aspects, parents, educators, and caregivers can establish a nurturing atmosphere that fosters the growth and development of individuals with autism.

Autistic individuals often exhibit a notable ability to focus on intricate details. This skill can lead to outstanding results in areas that demand meticulousness and exactness. As an expert in animal behavior, Temple Grandin has frequently discussed her keen observation skills, which allow her to detect even the smallest details that may go unnoticed by others. Her expertise in this area has greatly contributed to her success in developing humane livestock handling systems. Grandin's meticulous approach enables her to identify and resolve issues in animal facilities that may go unnoticed by others, resulting in a substantial enhancement of livestock welfare. Acknowledging and utilizing this particular aptitude can open up opportunities in professions such as engineering, quality control, and research, where a meticulous focus on details is highly prized.

Autistic individuals often demonstrate exceptional abilities in the area of memory. Certain individuals possess exceptional recall abilities, commonly known as eidetic memory, enabling them to accurately remember intricate information. This skill is highly valuable in academic and professional settings that depend on the comprehension and utilization of intricate information. As an example, Satoshi Tajiri, the creator of Pokémon, utilized his remarkable memory and unwavering dedication to his passions to cultivate one of the most prosperous entertainment franchises in history. By recognizing and providing support for this aptitude, we can assist individuals with autism in excelling in areas that require excellent memory capabilities, such as history, languages, and data analysis.

Autistic individuals often possess a notable aptitude for pattern recognition. The capacity to identify patterns and regularities in data can prove to be extremely beneficial in a wide range of fields, such as mathematics, music, and computer science. John Elder Robison, a renowned author and advocate in the field, has shared insights into his innate ability to discern patterns and systems. This exceptional skill has played a pivotal role in his successful endeavors in electronics and special effects. By promoting the exploration and development of pattern recognition skills in autistic individuals, opportunities for careers in fields such as cryptography, software development, and financial analysis can be unlocked. These industries highly appreciate and value this particular ability.

Specialized interests, commonly known as "special interests" in the autism community, can also serve as a valuable source of strength. It is common for individuals with autism to develop strong and focused interests in particular subjects, often acquiring a level of expertise that exceeds that of their peers. These interests can serve as a source of purpose and motivation, inspiring individuals to achieve excellence in their chosen fields. As an illustration, Dr. Stephen Shore, a professor and advocate who is autistic, has transformed his enduring love for music into a thriving vocation in the fields of education and autism advocacy. By promoting and fostering these specific interests, we can assist individuals with autism in cultivating specialized knowledge that can pave the way for rewarding and prosperous professional paths.

To effectively understand and foster these strengths, it is important to shift one's perspective from solely focusing on weaknesses to acknowledging and developing existing abilities. An essential aspect of fostering resilience is adopting a strengths-based approach, which aids in the development of a positive self-image and a sense of competence for autistic individuals. The process entails establishing inclusive environments that embrace and honor the diversity of neurological conditions, allowing individuals on the autism spectrum to leverage their unique abilities in order to surmount obstacles and attain their objectives.

Establishing such environments typically involves developing individualized education plans that address the specific strengths and requirements of students with autism. It is recommended that the plans include strategies that take advantage of the individuals' abilities. For instance, visual aids can be used to cater to those with strong visual-spatial skills, while hands-on activities can be incorporated for kinesthetic learners. By customizing educational methods to suit the unique strengths of each student, we can improve the quality of learning experiences and achieve better outcomes for individuals with autism.

In order to promote resilience, it is important to offer autistic individuals the chance to enhance their skills in practical environments. One option is to explore internships, volunteer opportunities, and mentorship programs that are in line with their interests and abilities. For instance, offering an internship in a research laboratory to a student who possesses exceptional analytical skills can be instrumental in helping them acquire invaluable experience and cultivate a sense of self-assurance in their capabilities. These opportunities not only emphasize the significance of their strengths but also offer practical applications that can pave the way for future career achievements.

Another crucial aspect of identifying and fostering strengths is social support. It is crucial for families, educators, and communities to actively support and foster the interests and abilities of autistic individuals. The self-esteem and motivation of individuals can be greatly influenced by the positive reinforcement, encouragement, and understanding they receive from those in their environment. For example, parents who actively support their child's interest in music by enrolling them in lessons and attending their performances can enhance the child's confidence and cultivate a sense of achievement.

In addition, promoting resilience by recognizing strengths also includes instructing individuals with autism on self-advocacy skills. It is crucial for their long-term success to empower individuals to effectively express their needs and preferences and to actively pursue environments that recognize and appreciate their strengths. Our services encompass the provision of information regarding individuals' rights, guidance in the development of efficient communication techniques, and the facilitation of opportunities for individuals to enhance their self-advocacy skills across different contexts.

In this context, it is crucial to emphasize the significance of community and connection. Being a member of a supportive community that values neurodiversity and promotes inclusion can greatly influence the resilience and well-being of individuals on the autism spectrum. Community programs, support groups, and social activities that are tailored to the interests and strengths of autistic individuals offer valuable opportunities for social interaction and personal development. For instance, clubs or groups that center around common interests, such as coding, art, or gaming, can foster a sense of belonging and serve as a platform for individuals on the autism spectrum to showcase their talents.

Recognizing and fostering the strengths and abilities of individuals on the autism spectrum is a crucial element in developing resilience. By redirecting our attention towards the strengths and capabilities of autistic individuals, we have the opportunity to establish nurturing environments that enable them to flourish. Acknowledging and fostering individuals' strengths in areas such as attention to detail, memory, pattern recognition, and specialized interests can result in notable personal and professional accomplishments. By implementing personalized education plans, providing real-world opportunities, offering social support, promoting self-advocacy, and creating inclusive communities, we can support autistic individuals in developing resilience, building confidence, and achieving success in their pursuits. The insights gained from these approaches have a positive impact on both autistic individuals and society as a whole, fostering inclusivity and appreciation for the diverse contributions of every member.

Fostering Self-Esteem and Confidence

Developing self-esteem and confidence in individuals with autism is crucial for cultivating resilience. Resilience is greatly influenced by an individual's self-worth and belief in their abilities. It is the ability to navigate and recover from adversity. Developing a strong sense of self-esteem and confidence is crucial for the personal growth and success of autistic individuals, who often face unique challenges and societal misunderstandings. This process entails comprehending their strengths, creating supportive environments, and fostering self-advocacy and independence.

Self-esteem is closely linked to an individual's self-perception and their perception of how others perceive them. The perception of autistic individuals can be shaped by societal attitudes, educational experiences, and family dynamics. There are frequently misunderstandings in society regarding autism, resulting in the stigmatization and exclusion of individuals. To address these negative perceptions, it is crucial to actively work towards changing the narrative to acknowledge and appreciate the distinct strengths and valuable contributions of individuals on the autism spectrum.

Assisting individuals on the autism spectrum in

acknowledging and embracing their strengths is a crucial aspect of promoting self-esteem. Every individual possesses a distinct range of abilities and aptitudes that, when recognized and cultivated, can serve as a foundation for personal satisfaction and self-assurance. For instance, individuals with autism often demonstrate a keen focus on details, a robust memory, and impressive skills in recognizing patterns. By emphasizing these strengths instead of weaknesses, we can assist them in developing a constructive self-perception.

The role of educational settings is crucial in this process. Inclusive education allows for the integration of autistic students with their neurotypical peers, fostering social interaction and promoting academic success. It is crucial that these environments prioritize inclusivity and provide personalized support to meet the unique needs of autistic students. This could potentially include the implementation of individualized education plans (IEPs) that focus on and enhance the student's strengths rather than solely addressing their challenges.

It is essential for teachers and educators to receive proper training in order to develop a comprehensive understanding of autism and effectively foster an inclusive and supportive classroom environment. It is essential to utilize positive reinforcement, acknowledge accomplishments, and provide constructive feedback. For example, acknowledging the exceptional memory of an autistic student in a history class or recognizing their analytical skills in a math lesson can help to strengthen their abilities and enhance their self-esteem. In addition, peer mentoring programs can be advantageous as they provide autistic students with guidance and support from older students. This can further enhance their confidence and social skills.

Family support plays a crucial role in nurturing self-esteem and confidence. The attitudes of families can have a profound impact on the self-perception of autistic individuals, as they are often the main source of emotional support. Parents and siblings who prioritize highlighting strengths, acknowledging accomplishments, and offering unwavering love and acceptance contribute to a supportive atmosphere that promotes a sense of self-value. Family members should prioritize educating themselves about autism to dispel any misconceptions and gain a deeper understanding of the unique experiences of their autistic loved ones.

Promoting autonomy is another vital element in fostering self-assurance and self-confidence. Autistic individuals, just like anyone else, require opportunities to explore their interests, exercise their decision-making abilities, and assume responsibilities. Structured activities that promote autonomy include managing a small project, participating in extracurricular activities, or volunteering. These experiences help individuals develop valuable life skills and foster a sense of achievement, which can contribute to an increased sense of self-worth.

Self-advocacy is a crucial skill that enables individuals on the autism spectrum to effectively communicate their needs, make well-informed choices, and assert their autonomy. Teaching self-advocacy entails assisting individuals in comprehending their rights, cultivating efficient communication strategies, and honing assertiveness in diverse environments. For instance, engaging in role-playing scenarios where individuals advocate for accommodations in educational or professional settings can enhance their self-assurance and equip them with the necessary skills for real-life situations. Autistic individuals who are able to effectively advocate for themselves are more likely to experience a sense of value and respect, leading to a positive impact on their self-esteem.

Community support and involvement are crucial factors in nurturing self-esteem and confidence. Creating inclusive communities that embrace diversity and foster acceptance is crucial for providing autistic individuals with a strong sense of belonging and validation. Community programs, such as social clubs, sports teams, and interest-based groups, provide valuable opportunities for individuals to engage in social interactions, enhance their skills, and celebrate their accomplishments. The design of these programs should prioritize creating an inclusive and accommodating environment, allowing individuals with autism to fully and comfortably engage.

The influence of media and popular culture on self-esteem and confidence is significant. Portraying autistic individuals in a positive light through movies, television, books, and online media has the potential to challenge prevailing stereotypes and offer valuable role models. Examining the accomplishments of accomplished individuals on the autism spectrum, such as Temple Grandin, Satoshi Tajiri, or Jessica-Jane Applegate, can serve as a source of inspiration and evidence that autism does not impede success. Accurate and respectful media portrayals of autism play a crucial role in cultivating a well-informed and accepting society. This, in turn, nurtures the self-esteem of individuals on the autism spectrum.

Ensuring access to mental health support is an essential component of this process. Autistic individuals frequently face elevated levels of anxiety, depression, and other mental health difficulties. These challenges often arise from factors such as social isolation, sensory overload, and the demands of navigating a world designed for neurotypical individuals. Having access to mental health services that are specifically designed to meet individual needs can offer valuable coping strategies and emotional support. Therapy, whether conducted on an individual or group basis, provides a secure environment for individuals with autism to delve into their emotions, cultivate resilience, and foster a healthy self-perception.

When promoting self-esteem and confidence, it is crucial to take a comprehensive approach that considers all aspects of an individual's life, particularly those with autism. It is crucial to prioritize the overall well-being of individuals by addressing their physical health needs through access to appropriate healthcare and nutrition. Additionally, fostering intellectual growth can be achieved by promoting education and encouraging lifelong learning. Lastly, it is important to support emotional health by cultivating strong relationships and providing access to mental health resources. By considering these factors, we can establish a thorough support system that fosters resilience and enables individuals with autism to live meaningful lives.

Developing self-esteem and confidence in individuals with autism is a complex undertaking that necessitates collaboration among families, educators, communities, and society at large. It is essential to acknowledge and appreciate individuals' strengths, create inclusive environments that offer support, foster independence, encourage self-advocacy, and guarantee access to mental health resources. These elements are vital to the success of this initiative. By establishing a strong sense of self-esteem and confidence, we provide autistic individuals with the necessary tools to overcome obstacles and reach their maximum capabilities. This not only benefits individuals personally but also enriches our communities, as we learn to value and embrace the diverse contributions of all individuals.

CHAPTER 3

OVERCOMING OBSTACLES

Practical Tips for Tackling Common Challenges

Confronting barriers is a fundamental aspect of existence, and for individuals with autism, this frequently entails distinct hurdles that necessitate pragmatic and considerate approaches. Addressing these prevalent challenges in a proficient manner can result in enhanced self-reliance, assurance, and overall welfare. It is crucial to provide practical tips for addressing these challenges, as they are not only important for autistic individuals but also for their families, caregivers, and educators who play a vital role in their support systems.

Sensory sensitivity is a significant and widespread challenge experienced by individuals with autism. Individuals with autism often have a heightened sensitivity to stimuli, such as loud noises, bright lights, or certain textures. This can result in sensory overload. In order to effectively manage this, it is of utmost importance to establish environments that are conducive to sensory needs. One approach is to utilize noise-canceling headphones in noisy environments, provide sunglasses or dim lighting for individuals who are sensitive to light, and offer clothing made from soft, comfortable fabrics. Implementing sensory breaks throughout the day can be beneficial, as they provide individuals with the opportunity to seek solace in a serene environment and alleviate stress.

Another common challenge that individuals often face is difficulty in communication. Individuals with autism may experience difficulties with verbal communication, interpreting nonverbal cues, and engaging in social interactions. Using alternative communication methods can offer significant advantages. Augmentative and alternative communication (AAC) devices, such as speech-generating devices or communication apps, offer a means of communication for individuals who are unable to speak. Utilizing visual aids, such as the picture exchange communication system (PECS), can be instrumental in effectively expressing one's needs and desires. In addition, incorporating the use of social stories can be beneficial for enhancing comprehension and ease in social interactions. Social stories are concise narratives that depict various social situations and provide guidance on appropriate behaviors and responses.

Autistic individuals often face difficulties in understanding social cues and norms, which can make navigating social situations particularly challenging for them. Structured social skills training offers valuable guidance. Engaging in role-playing exercises can be a valuable tool for individuals to enhance their social skills and effectively navigate real-life social situations. In addition, incorporating social activities that are in line with their interests can provide organic chances for socializing. For example, participating in clubs or groups that center around a particular hobby or passion can enhance social interactions, making them more comfortable and meaningful.

It is widely observed that autistic individuals often experience challenges related to executive functioning, specifically in areas such as planning, organization, and time management. To tackle these challenges, establishing well-organized routines and providing precise, sequential instructions can be highly beneficial. Visual schedules that outline daily activities can offer a clear structure and help individuals anticipate and manage their day with ease. Utilizing tools such as planners, apps, and timers can be highly beneficial for effectively managing tasks and meeting deadlines. Dividing tasks into smaller, more manageable steps and incorporating regular breaks can also improve focus and productivity.

Individuals with autism frequently encounter difficulties when transitioning between activities or environments. Effective preparation for transitions can help alleviate these challenges by utilizing clear communication and visual aids. Using countdown timers or visual timers can be beneficial in helping individuals grasp the amount of time left before a transition takes place. Social stories can be utilized to provide a clear and objective description of what individuals can anticipate during a transition, effectively minimizing feelings of uncertainty and anxiety. Offering a transitional object, such as a beloved toy or a comforting item, can provide extra reassurance.

Responses to overwhelming situations, such as meltdowns and shutdowns, can be distressing for both autistic individuals and those around them. It is crucial to identify triggers and early warning signs in order to effectively manage these episodes. It is crucial to maintain a calm and supportive environment during a meltdown or shutdown.

Methods such as deep pressure therapy, the utilization of weighted blankets, or the implementation of deep breathing exercises have been found to be effective in promoting relaxation and reducing stress on the nervous system. After an episode, it is crucial to create a supportive environment for healing and to have open conversations about the factors that contributed to the episode. This approach can be instrumental in minimizing the likelihood of similar incidents in the future.

Autistic students often face distinct challenges in educational settings, necessitating customized support to ensure their academic success. It is crucial to implement individualized education programs (IEPs) that address the unique needs and strengths of each individual. It is important to include accommodations in these plans, such as extended time on tests, the option to take breaks, and the use of assistive technology. Effective collaboration among teachers, special education professionals, and families is crucial to ensuring a cohesive and comprehensive approach to support. In addition, creating an inclusive classroom environment that values diversity can improve the learning experience for students with autism.

Securing employment and achieving independent living are important milestones that can present unique challenges. Offering vocational training and job coaching can effectively equip individuals on the autism spectrum with the necessary skills and support to thrive in the workforce. We offer a comprehensive training program that covers interview practice, resume building, and on-the-job support. Identifying careers that are in line with one's strengths and interests can result in more fulfilling employment opportunities. Life skills training, including cooking, budgeting, and using public transportation, is essential for individuals seeking to live independently. Supported living arrangements or assisted living communities offer individuals the opportunity to maintain their independence while receiving the necessary support they need.

The support for autistic individuals often overlooks the importance of mental health. There is a notable prevalence of anxiety, depression, and other mental health issues within the autistic community. It is crucial to have access to mental health professionals who possess a deep understanding of autism. Therapeutic approaches, including cognitive-behavioral therapy (CBT), can be modified to effectively address the unique requirements of individuals with autism. Promoting regular physical activity, mindfulness practices, and hobbies can also enhance overall well-being.

Having a strong network of family support is crucial when it comes to overcoming obstacles. It is important for families to acquire knowledge about autism in order to offer well-informed and empathetic care. Support groups for parents and siblings provide valuable resources and foster a sense of community. Respite care services are crucial as they provide caregivers with a much-needed opportunity to recharge and take a break.

It is crucial to foster community awareness and acceptance in order to establish a nurturing environment for individuals with autism. Efforts in advocacy should prioritize the promotion of understanding and inclusion within a broader society. These initiatives may include raising awareness, implementing autism-friendly policies, and promoting inclusive practices in public spaces. Creating a community that embraces neurodiversity can lead to a more supportive and empowering environment for individuals on the autism spectrum.

There are a wide range of technological tools available that can help individuals overcome their daily challenges. There is a wide availability of apps that are designed to assist with communication, organization, and social skills. Virtual reality (VR) is currently being studied as a potential tool to assist individuals with autism in practicing social interactions and managing anxiety-inducing situations within a controlled environment. With the ongoing advancement of technology, it is expected that there will be a steady stream of innovative solutions to further assist the autistic community.

To address the common challenges experienced by individuals with autism, it is essential to adopt a comprehensive approach that encompasses practical strategies, conducive environments, and a robust support network comprising family members, educators, and community stakeholders. Through the implementation of sensory-friendly practices, alternative communication methods, structured routines, and social skills training, a solid foundation for success can be established. In addition, it is crucial to address mental health needs, offer vocational training, and promote community acceptance as essential elements. By leveraging these collective endeavors, we can provide support to individuals with autism, enabling them to effectively overcome challenges, develop their ability to bounce back, and ultimately reach their utmost capabilities. This comprehensive approach not only benefits individuals with autism but also enhances our communities by promoting diversity, comprehension, and inclusivity.

Stories of Perseverance and Triumph

Perseverance and triumph are significant concepts that hold great meaning in the human experience, especially when it comes to overcoming challenges. Autistic individuals often face a multitude of challenges on their path to achieving their goals. The stories of perseverance and triumph underscore the resilience of these individuals and emphasize the crucial role of support systems in enabling them to reach their maximum potential. Through an examination of these narratives, a deeper comprehension of the distinct obstacles and remarkable achievements of individuals on the autism spectrum is attained. This offers inspiration and valuable insights for those encountering comparable difficulties.

An example of such a story is that of Temple Grandin, a well-known animal behaviorist and advocate for autism. Grandin was diagnosed with autism during a period when there was limited understanding of the condition. As a result, she encountered notable difficulties in social interactions and communication. Her journey exemplifies the strength of unwavering determination. Grandin's unwavering dedication and deep understanding of animals propelled her to transform livestock handling practices, enhancing their compassion and effectiveness. Thanks to her unique perspective, which she attributes to her autism, she was able to create groundbreaking equipment and systems. Grandin overcame skepticism and discrimination through her unwavering determination and the support of her family and mentors, ultimately establishing herself as a prominent figure in her field. This story highlights the significance of acknowledging and fostering individual strengths, along with the influence of a supportive environment on overcoming challenges.

Dr. Stephen Shore serves as an exemplary figure in the field of special education. As an autistic professor and a highly respected speaker, he has garnered international recognition for his expertise. Shore experienced a delay in developing verbal communication skills, not speaking until the age of four. Additionally, they encountered notable difficulties in social interaction. His parents were recommended to consider institutionalizing him; however, they made the decision to foster and develop his abilities instead. Shore's communication skills were developed through intensive therapy and education, allowing him to pursue his academic interests. Currently, he possesses a doctoral degree and is a well-known advocate for raising awareness and promoting acceptance of autism. Shore's journey demonstrates the power of early intervention, personalized education, and a strong support system in turning challenges into opportunities for success. His work serves as a source of inspiration and education for others regarding the capabilities of individuals with autism.

Jessica Jane Applegate, a British Paralympic swimmer, presents a captivating narrative of overcoming challenges. Applegate was diagnosed with autism at the age of 15. Throughout their journey, they encountered various challenges, such as sensory sensitivities and the demands of competitive sports. In spite of the obstacles she faced, she directed her attention and resolve towards swimming, achieving remarkable feats and securing a gold medal at the 2012 London Paralympics. The individual's achievements in swimming serve as a compelling testament to the significance of persistence and the rewards that come with pursuing one's true calling. Applegate's story underscores the significance of sports and physical activity in bolstering confidence, enhancing mental well-being, and cultivating a sense of accomplishment among individuals on the autism spectrum.

The story of Daniel Tammet, an individual with autism, serves as a compelling example of the remarkable capabilities that can be found within the autism spectrum. Tammet possesses a remarkable aptitude for executing intricate mathematical computations and acquiring new languages with remarkable speed. Tammet has overcome challenges related to social interactions and sensory sensitivities, utilizing his exceptional cognitive abilities to achieve success as an author and public speaker. The memoir, "Born on a Blue Day," offers a valuable perspective on living with autism, providing insight into the author's experiences and challenges. The accomplishments of Tammet in academia and literature serve as a testament to the potential of individuals on the autism spectrum to thrive in various domains when their unique abilities are acknowledged and nurtured.

The narratives of resilience and victory highlight not only personal achievements but also the collaborative endeavors of families, educators, and communities. Support systems play a crucial role in assisting autistic individuals to overcome obstacles. It is crucial to prioritize early diagnosis and intervention, along with the implementation of personalized education plans and the creation of inclusive environments, in order to effectively promote resilience. In addition, raising awareness and fostering acceptance of autism in society contributes to the creation of a more inclusive world, enabling individuals with autism to flourish.

Education is a crucial factor in the success of these stories. Inclusive education allows for the integration of autistic students with their neurotypical peers, fostering both social interaction and academic development. Teachers who possess a deep understanding of autism and implement personalized strategies can have a profound impact. Visual supports, structured routines, and sensory accommodations have been found to enhance the learning experience for students with autism. Recognizing and embracing the diversity of neurodiverse students in educational settings fosters a sense of confidence and self-esteem, empowering them to explore and develop their unique interests and talents.

Community involvement is an essential factor to consider. Creating inclusive communities that prioritize diversity and foster acceptance is crucial for providing autistic individuals with a strong sense of belonging and validation. Community programs, such as social clubs, sports teams, and interest-based groups, provide valuable opportunities for individuals to engage in social interaction, enhance their skills, and celebrate their accomplishments. Creating an inclusive environment that values and supports individuals on the autism spectrum is crucial for their personal and professional growth.

In addition, it is crucial to emphasize the importance of self-advocacy and independence when it comes to overcoming obstacles. When individuals with autism are given the tools to communicate their needs, make choices, and stand up for themselves, they are more capable of overcoming obstacles. Teaching self-advocacy skills entails assisting individuals in comprehending their rights, cultivating efficient communication strategies, and honing assertiveness in diverse settings. This process of empowerment instills a sense of confidence and agency, allowing individuals on the autism spectrum to assume control over their lives and accomplish their aspirations.

It is crucial to prioritize mental health support throughout this journey. It is common for individuals with autism to experience elevated levels of anxiety, depression, and other mental health concerns. It is imperative to have access to mental health services that possess a comprehensive understanding of autism. Therapeutic approaches, such as cognitive-behavioral therapy (CBT), can be tailored to address the specific requirements of individuals with autism. Promoting consistent engagement in physical activity, mindfulness practices, and hobbies can enhance overall well-being and resilience.

Employment and independent living are important achievements for individuals on the autism spectrum. By engaging in vocational training and job coaching, individuals can acquire the necessary skills to succeed in the workforce. Additionally, supported living arrangements offer a harmonious blend of independence and essential support. Identifying careers that are in line with one's strengths and interests can lead to a wide range of fulfilling employment opportunities. These accomplishments in employment and independent living serve as a testament to the value of persistence and the influence of a strong support system.

Accounts of resilience, support, and empowerment among individuals with autism are compelling stories that underscore the significance of perseverance and triumph. Through the acknowledgement and support of their unique abilities, the creation of inclusive surroundings, and the encouragement of self-advocacy, we can assist individuals with autism in surmounting challenges and reaching their utmost capabilities. These stories have the power to inspire individuals who are facing similar challenges while also playing a role in fostering a more inclusive and understanding society. Through the adoption of neurodiversity and the cultivation of an inclusive culture, we can establish a society where individuals are empowered to flourish.

CHAPTER 4

STRATEGIES FOR PARENTS AND CAREGIVERS

Supporting Your Child's Emotional Growth

Supporting the emotional development of your child is an essential responsibility for parents and caregivers, particularly those with autistic children. The process of emotional growth involves the advancement of a child's capacity to comprehend, articulate, and regulate their emotions. This, in turn, promotes resilience, self-awareness, and social competence. Considering the distinct obstacles encountered by children with autism, it is crucial to implement strategies that are effective and specifically designed to meet their individual needs. This holistic approach not only improves their emotional well-being but also empowers them to navigate life's challenges with self-assurance and poise.

Gaining a comprehensive grasp of the fundamental principles of emotional growth is an essential initial step. The process of emotional growth in children entails the gradual refinement of emotional intelligence. This encompasses the ability to identify and acknowledge one's own emotions, comprehend the emotions of others, and react to emotional stimuli in a suitable manner. Autistic children may encounter additional complexities in this process as a result of variations in social communication and sensory processing. Thus, it is crucial for parents and caregivers to implement strategies that effectively cater to these distinct needs, creating an environment that is both supportive and nurturing.

An essential strategy involves establishing a secure and consistent environment. Children with autism typically benefit from a structured and consistent environment, as unexpected changes can cause feelings of anxiety and difficulty managing emotions. Creating a consistent daily schedule that incorporates designated times for meals, activities, and rest can contribute to a feeling of stability and reassurance. Visual schedules and social stories are highly effective tools that can greatly assist children in comprehending and anticipating upcoming events, thereby mitigating feelings of uncertainty and stress. To create an environment conducive to emotional growth, parents and caregivers should aim to minimize unexpected events and maintain stability.

Effective communication is an essential element. Verbal communication can be a significant challenge for many children with autism, highlighting the importance of investigating alternative methods. Augmentative and Alternative Communication (AAC) devices, picture exchange communication systems (PECS), and sign language can serve as effective tools to facilitate children's expression of their needs and emotions. Promoting the utilization of these tools in daily interactions aids in children feeling acknowledged and comprehended, cultivating a favorable emotional bond with their caregivers.

Developing a comprehensive range of emotional words is of equal significance. It is important for children to have a vocabulary to express their emotions, as this enables them to communicate their feelings effectively rather than resorting to disruptive behavior. Parents and caregivers can demonstrate this behavior by clearly identifying their own emotions in a specific situation. For example, stating "I am experiencing happiness because we are engaging in quality time together" or "I am feeling frustration due to the deviation from our planned course of action" offers a precise illustration for children. Engaging with literature that delves into a range of emotions and engaging in thoughtful discussions about the characters' feelings can further develop one's emotional literacy. Over time, this practice enables children to cultivate a strong vocabulary that allows them to express their emotions in a more precise and constructive manner.

Active listening is a highly effective technique that showcases empathy and validation. It is of utmost importance to acknowledge a child's emotions, whether they are expressed verbally or through behavior, without passing judgment. One way to address this is by using clear and objective statements, such as "I acknowledge your emotions and understand that you are feeling upset" or "Based on what you've shared, it appears that you are experiencing sadness." These responses provide validation for the child's experience, creating a sense of understanding and support. This validation serves as the initial step in assisting individuals in processing and managing their emotions.

Developing effective emotion regulation skills is crucial for effectively managing and coping with stress and anxiety. Providing autistic children with techniques such as deep breathing, progressive muscle relaxation, and mindfulness can equip them with effective tools to manage moments of distress. Regular practice and incorporation into one's daily routine can make these techniques more accessible, especially during challenging times. In addition, it is recommended to establish a designated area at home where children can go to relax and calm themselves. This space should be equipped with sensory-friendly items such as soft pillows, weighted blankets, and calming visuals.

Social interactions provide a platform for individuals to experience emotional development. Children with autism may face difficulties in social situations. However, with appropriate support, these situations can be transformed into valuable learning and growth experiences. Parents and caregivers can promote social interactions by organizing playdates or group activities with peers who have common interests. Participating in organized social activities, such as joining a club or a team, offers a secure setting for honing social skills. Engaging in role-playing activities at home can effectively equip children with the necessary skills to navigate real-life social interactions. By immersing themselves in various social scenarios, children can gain a deeper understanding of social cues and appropriate responses.

The development of one's emotional well-being is strongly correlated with their level of self-esteem and self-acceptance. It is important for all children, including those with autism, to experience a sense of worth and acceptance for their unique qualities. Recognizing their accomplishments, regardless of size, enhances their self-assurance and strengthens their constructive self-perception. Parents and caregivers should prioritize their child's strengths and interests, offering them ample opportunities to thrive in these particular areas. Utilizing positive reinforcement, such as offering praise and rewards, can effectively encourage desired behaviors and foster a sense of accomplishment.

It is crucial to provide education to siblings and extended family members regarding autism and the specific requirements of a child with autism. An environment that promotes neurodiversity within the family can greatly contribute to a child's emotional development. Encouraging siblings to engage in activities that foster bonding and understanding can promote a sense of unity and support within the family.

Seeking assistance from a qualified professional can greatly contribute to the development of emotional well-being. Professionals who have expertise in autism can offer specialized interventions and support, including therapists, counselors, and special educators. There are several approaches that can assist children in developing emotional regulation and social skills, such as Applied Behavior Analysis (ABA), Cognitive Behavioral Therapy (CBT), and play therapy. It is recommended that parents and caregivers actively search for these resources and work together with professionals to develop a thorough support plan that is specifically designed to meet their child's individual needs.

Aside from professional assistance, families can also benefit from the wealth of information and emotional support provided by community resources like support groups and advocacy organizations. Engaging with fellow parents and caregivers who have faced similar situations can offer valuable guidance, support, and a feeling of belonging. Additionally, these networks have the ability to promote improved services and support systems within the wider community, thus making a valuable contribution towards fostering inclusivity in society.

Self-care for parents and caregivers is crucial. Assisting in the emotional development of a child with autism can be quite challenging, necessitating caregivers to prioritize their own emotional and physical health. Taking regular breaks, pursuing hobbies, seeking support from loved ones, and seeking professional counseling when necessary can assist in preserving one's resilience and capacity to provide optimal care for their child.

Supporting the emotional growth of a child with autism necessitates a comprehensive and empathetic approach. Parents and caregivers play a crucial role in promoting their child's emotional well-being. This can be achieved by establishing a safe and predictable environment, improving communication, developing emotional vocabulary, practicing active listening, teaching emotion regulation skills, facilitating social interactions, and nurturing self-esteem. In addition, utilizing professional assistance and community resources while also prioritizing personal well-being guarantees a well-rounded and efficient approach. By implementing these initiatives, children with autism can cultivate the necessary emotional strength and self-assurance to effectively navigate the obstacles of life and reach their maximum capabilities.

Creating a Nurturing Environment

Establishing a supportive atmosphere is a crucial element in fostering the development of self-assured and accomplished children with autism. Parents and caregivers face the task of comprehending their children's distinct requirements and applying methods that support their growth, emotional health, and social integration. Creating a nurturing environment for autistic children extends beyond meeting their basic needs. It entails establishing a space where they feel secure, appreciated, and encouraged, empowering them to flourish and achieve their utmost capabilities.

First and foremost, it is crucial to have a comprehensive understanding of the sensory needs of children with autism. Autistic individuals often experience either heightened or diminished sensitivities to sensory stimuli, including light, sound, touch, and smell. The sensitivities mentioned can have a considerable impact on individuals' comfort and their ability to function in different environments. For instance, a child may experience difficulties with certain noises or textures. Establishing a sensory-friendly environment in your home can assist in addressing these challenges. Consider implementing strategies such as utilizing gentle lighting, offering noise-canceling headphones, or integrating sensory-friendly materials into clothing and bedding. These adjustments contribute to the reduction of sensory overload and the creation of a more comfortable and predictable environment for the child.

Creating a nurturing environment requires the establishment of routines and predictability. Children with autism often benefit from having a consistent routine and structure in their daily lives. This helps them feel secure and allows them to better anticipate what will happen throughout their day. Establishing consistent daily schedules for activities like meals, playtime, and bedtime can have numerous benefits. Visual schedules or planners can be effective tools for communicating routines to the child, enabling them to anticipate upcoming events and transitions visually. This predictability decreases anxiety and assists children in feeling more in control of their environment.

Clear and concise communication is essential for creating a supportive and productive atmosphere. Verbal communication can pose challenges for many children with autism, emphasizing the importance for parents and caregivers to explore alternative methods of communication. Devices such as augmentative and alternative communication (AAC), picture exchange communication systems (PECS), and sign language are highly valuable tools for effectively expressing needs, wants, and emotions. In addition, engaging in active listening and being attentive to non-verbal cues can enhance the connection between parents and their children, promoting a greater level of comprehension and trust.

Providing adequate emotional support is crucial to fostering the development of an autistic child. It is important for parents and caregivers to establish an environment that recognizes and affirms emotions. It is important to develop the ability to identify and label emotions, both in oneself and in one's children, in order to enhance emotional literacy. For example, when a child is upset, caregivers can acknowledge their emotions by saying, "I can see that you are feeling sad. Would you like to discuss the matter at hand? This method facilitates the development of emotional intelligence in children by assisting them in recognizing and articulating their emotions. In addition, it is important to create a secure environment where children can seek solace when they feel overwhelmed. This can be achieved by setting up a peaceful area equipped with soothing items like blankets and soft toys. Such a space can assist children in regulating their emotions and effectively managing their feelings.

Developing a strong sense of self-worth and assurance is

crucial to creating a supportive atmosphere. It is important to recognize and appreciate the value of autistic children, just as we do for all children. Recognizing and acknowledging their accomplishments, regardless of size, while emphasizing their strengths instead of their obstacles, can greatly enhance their self-confidence. Nurturing their interests and offering chances for them to explore and cultivate their talents cultivates a feeling of achievement and satisfaction. Utilizing positive reinforcement, such as praise and rewards, can effectively enhance motivation and strengthen desirable behaviors.

Another crucial element to consider is social interaction. Autistic children often face difficulties in social situations, but these interactions play a vital role in their overall development. Parents and caregivers can enhance social interactions by organizing playdates or group activities that correspond to the child's interests and abilities. Engaging in structured social opportunities, such as joining clubs or participating in community programs, offers a secure and encouraging environment for honing social skills. Engaging in role-playing activities at home can be beneficial for children as it helps them develop their social skills and boost their self-assurance in real-life situations.

Education plays a crucial role in establishing a supportive atmosphere. Education settings that promote inclusivity provide a valuable environment for autistic children to learn alongside their neurotypical peers. This inclusive approach not only fosters socialization but also facilitates academic growth. Well-informed educators who possess expertise in autism and implement personalized strategies have the potential to make a substantial impact. Some possible strategies to consider are incorporating visual aids, allocating additional time for tasks, or permitting breaks to help manage sensory overload. It is important for parents and caregivers to work together with teachers and school staff to ensure that their child's educational needs are effectively addressed. This collaboration involves advocating for any necessary accommodations and support.

Active participation and assistance from the community are crucial. Connecting with other families of autistic children through support groups or community organizations can offer valuable resources, advice, and emotional support. Furthermore, these connections have the potential to cultivate a strong sense of community and belonging, effectively mitigating feelings of isolation. In addition, promoting increased awareness and acceptance of autism within the wider community can help create a more inclusive environment where individuals with autism are treated with respect and appreciation.

Support services, such as occupational therapy, speech therapy, and behavioral therapy, are essential in creating a nurturing environment. These services provide targeted interventions that address specific challenges and promote the child's development. It is recommended that parents and caregivers actively search for these resources and collaborate closely with professionals to develop a comprehensive support plan that is specifically designed for their child's individual needs. Consistent monitoring and adjustments to this plan are necessary to ensure its ongoing effectiveness and responsiveness to the child's changing needs.

Ensuring the well-being of parents and caregivers is an essential aspect of fostering a nurturing environment. It is crucial for caregivers to prioritize their own well-being when caring for an autistic child, as this responsibility can be demanding and emotionally challenging. It is important to consider seeking support from friends and family, taking breaks when necessary, and participating in activities that promote relaxation and enjoyment. When caregivers prioritize their own physical and emotional well-being, they are more capable of offering the consistent and empathetic assistance that their child requires.

Establishing an environment conducive to the well-being of children with autism requires a comprehensive strategy that encompasses their sensory, emotional, social, and educational requirements. To create a nurturing environment for autistic children, it is important for parents and caregivers to comprehend and address their specific challenges. This can be achieved through the establishment of consistent routines, promoting open and effective communication, and providing emotional support. By implementing these strategies, parents and caregivers can ensure that autistic children feel secure, appreciated, and empowered. In addition, utilizing community resources, professional support services, and self-care strategies guarantees a comprehensive and long-lasting approach to fostering their development. By implementing these initiatives, children with autism can acquire the necessary resilience, confidence, and abilities to effectively navigate their surroundings, ultimately resulting in a satisfying and empowered existence.

CHAPTER 5

COMMUNITY AND CONNECTION

The Importance of Social Support

Social support plays a crucial role in promoting resilience and well-being among individuals in the autistic community. Individuals on the autism spectrum often face difficulties when it comes to navigating social interactions and establishing meaningful connections. Nevertheless, a robust support network can have a profound impact on individuals, offering emotional validation, practical assistance, and a feeling of inclusion. This network expands beyond immediate family to encompass friends, peers, mentors, educators, and community organizations, all of whom have significant roles in cultivating a sense of community and connection.

Social support plays a crucial role in mitigating the impact of stress and adversity. Individuals with autism often encounter various challenges, such as communication difficulties, sensory sensitivities, and navigating social norms. Having a network of understanding and accepting individuals can help alleviate these challenges and validate their experiences. Social support is crucial during challenging times, providing individuals with a trusted confidant, a mentor, or a supportive community. These sources of support offer a lifeline, offering a non-judgmental ear, guidance, encouragement, and a space to share experiences.

Emotional support is a crucial component of social support, playing a vital role in providing assistance and comfort. Autistic individuals may experience increased levels of anxiety, depression, and feelings of isolation, especially when they perceive a lack of understanding or inclusion. Receiving support from a compassionate individual who acknowledges their emotions, demonstrates understanding, and creates a secure environment for open communication can greatly influence their mental health and overall well-being. This validation provides individuals with a sense of being acknowledged, listened to, and comprehended, which in turn lessens feelings of seclusion and promotes a feeling of being connected.

Practical support is highly valuable. Individuals with autism may benefit from support in various aspects of their daily lives, including tasks like household chores, schedule management, and navigating public spaces. Having a support network that provides practical assistance can help reduce stress and allow individuals to concentrate on their strengths and interests. This could include family members assisting with household responsibilities, friends offering transportation assistance, or professionals delivering specialized services customized to their requirements.

Effective social support is essential for fostering social inclusion and integration. Autistic individuals frequently encounter obstacles to social participation, such as stigma, discrimination, and a lack of comprehension. Nevertheless, individuals who have access to supportive social networks are more inclined to actively participate in social activities, establish meaningful friendships, and engage in various community events. These interactions offer valuable chances for individuals to learn, develop skills, and build meaningful relationships, ultimately enhancing their overall quality of life.

Autistic individuals can greatly benefit from peer support. Establishing connections with individuals who have comparable experiences and difficulties can cultivate a feeling of camaraderie and shared understanding. Peer support groups provide individuals with a platform to share personal stories, exchange valuable advice, and foster meaningful friendships rooted in shared interests and experiences. These groups offer a sense of validation and belonging, empowering individuals to embrace their identity and navigate the world with confidence.

Furthermore, mentorship can provide invaluable guidance and support in addition to peer assistance. Accessing mentors who have experience in a similar field can provide valuable guidance, encouragement, and practical advice. Mentors offer valuable guidance on navigating social situations, pursuing educational and career goals, and advocating for one's needs. They exemplify the qualities of role models and serve as a source of inspiration, showcasing the potential to overcome challenges and attain success within the autistic community.

Educators and professionals have a significant role in providing social support. Teachers who possess expertise in autism and utilize inclusive teaching practices establish a nurturing educational setting conducive to the success of autistic students. Through a comprehensive understanding of students' distinct abilities and obstacles, educators can customize their teaching methods to address individual requirements, encourage inclusivity, and cultivate a sense of belonging. Professionals in healthcare, therapy, and social services are equipped to provide specialized support and resources to assist autistic individuals in reaching their goals and effectively navigating the challenges of life.

Community organizations and advocacy groups play a crucial role in providing social support. These organizations offer a variety of services and resources, such as support groups, informational workshops, recreational activities, and advocacy initiatives. These organizations play a crucial role in fostering social connections, promoting self-advocacy, and empowering autistic individuals to actively engage in their communities by facilitating connections with peers and professionals. In addition, they have a crucial role in increasing awareness, addressing stigma, and advocating for policies and programs that benefit the autistic community as a whole.

Family support plays a crucial role in promoting the overall well-being of individuals with autism. Family members who offer unwavering love, acceptance, and support create a nurturing atmosphere that fosters the growth and development of individuals with autism. Family members can provide practical assistance, emotional support, and act as advocates for their loved ones. Through promoting transparent dialogue, acknowledging accomplishments, and embracing the unique perspectives of neurodiverse individuals, families play a vital role in enhancing the overall resilience and well-being of those with autism.

Support from others plays a crucial role in promoting resilience and well-being among individuals in the autistic community. Supportive social networks are essential for promoting social inclusion, fostering self-advocacy, and empowering autistic individuals to lead fulfilling lives. These networks provide emotional validation, practical assistance, peer connections, mentorship, and advocacy. By acknowledging the significance of social support and allocating resources to foster supportive relationships and community resources, we can establish a more inclusive society. This will ensure that all individuals, irrespective of neurodiversity, are given the chance to flourish.

Building a Network of Encouragement

Building a network of support is crucial for cultivating a strong sense of community and connection, especially when it comes to providing assistance to individuals, including those with autism, as they navigate life's obstacles. This network provides a strong support system, offering validation and motivation to individuals, enabling them to achieve their goals, overcome challenges, and succeed in both their personal and professional pursuits. This network fosters a culture of encouragement that uplifts and inspires its members. Positive reinforcement, empathy, and shared experiences are utilized to cultivate resilience, confidence, and a sense of belonging.

The foundation of establishing a network of encouragement lies in fostering supportive relationships. The relationships are marked by a sense of mutual respect, empathy, and trust, fostering a secure and supportive atmosphere where individuals are appreciated and comprehended. Having a strong network of connections, such as friends, family members, mentors, colleagues, or members of a support group, can be a valuable source of strength and encouragement during challenging periods. Through providing attentive support, practical aid, and words of motivation, members of this network play a vital role in uplifting and empowering each other.

Efficient communication plays a crucial role in establishing a supportive network. Effective communication promotes mutual understanding, empathy, and connection, allowing individuals to articulate their needs, share their experiences, and provide support to others. Active listening, acknowledging emotions, and providing constructive feedback are essential elements of successful communication within this network. By fostering an environment of open dialogue and respectful communication, individuals can cultivate stronger connections and enhance their support networks.

Understanding and compassion are essential elements of fostering motivation. When individuals within a network exhibit empathy, they possess the ability to comprehend and participate in the emotions of others, providing compassion, validation, and support. Empathy is a crucial factor in creating a sense of connection and belonging by making individuals feel seen, heard, and understood. Recognizing and affirming the experiences of others can offer valuable support that motivates and empowers those who require it.

Utilizing positive reinforcement can be highly effective in establishing a supportive network. Through the provision of praise, recognition, and support, individuals have the ability to motivate and inspire others, enabling them to achieve their utmost potential. Positive reinforcement plays a crucial role in fostering a culture of encouragement within the network. It involves celebrating achievements, acknowledging progress, and offering words of affirmation to reinforce positive behaviors. This support enhances confidence, cultivates self-assurance, and enables individuals to pursue their objectives with unwavering determination and resilience.

Sharing personal experiences and stories of resilience can have a profound impact on fostering a supportive network. By sharing their personal struggles, challenges, and triumphs, individuals within the network foster a sense of solidarity and connection with others who may be encountering similar obstacles. Through the act of sharing their personal experiences, individuals provide a source of hope, inspiration, and practical guidance to those who may be facing similar challenges. This serves as a reminder that they are not alone in their struggles and that there is always the potential for a more positive and promising tomorrow.

Having a mentor is an important aspect of establishing a supportive network. Mentors offer valuable guidance, support, and wisdom derived from their own experiences and expertise. They provide insightful advice to individuals who are navigating similar paths, helping them along their journey. Mentors play a crucial role in guiding individuals to set goals, overcome obstacles, and achieve success in their personal and professional lives. By serving as role models and advocates, mentors empower others to reach their full potential. Mentorship plays a crucial role in cultivating a strong sense of community and fostering meaningful connections. It provides individuals with the opportunity to learn from one another and offer support for their personal growth and development.

Support groups are essential for establishing a network of encouragement. These groups offer a platform for individuals to connect with others who have similar experiences and challenges, providing empathy, validation, and practical advice. Support groups for parents of autistic children, individuals with disabilities, or survivors of trauma offer a vital sense of community and belonging, which is crucial for fostering resilience and well-being. By participating in these groups, individuals can gain strength, encouragement, and a sense of hope for the future through the sharing of experiences and mutual support.

Creating inclusive communities and organizations is crucial for fostering a supportive network. Through the establishment of inclusive environments that value diversity and recognize the distinct abilities and talents of every individual, these communities cultivate a strong sense of belonging and empowerment. Inclusive communities create an environment where individuals can thrive, whether it's a workplace that values diversity and promotes collaboration, a school that supports students with disabilities, or a neighborhood that welcomes individuals from all walks of life. These communities provide a supportive and nurturing atmosphere.

Establishing a network of support is crucial for cultivating a strong sense of community and connection, especially when it comes to assisting individuals in navigating life's obstacles. By fostering strong connections, employing clear and open communication, demonstrating empathy, offering constructive feedback, promoting shared experiences, providing mentorship, facilitating support groups, and cultivating inclusive communities, individuals have the ability to establish a culture of encouragement that motivates and uplifts each other. Through providing assistance, affirmation, and encouragement, members of this network empower one another to overcome challenges, pursue their aspirations, and excel in both personal and professional pursuits. Thanks to the strong and resilient network, individuals receive the necessary encouragement and support to confidently navigate life's challenges.

CHAPTER 6

FUTURE PLANNING

Preparing for Adulthood and Independence

Planning for the future and achieving independence is a crucial journey for individuals, including those on the autism spectrum. It is a significant aspect of preparing for adulthood and taking steps towards self-sufficiency. This transition represents a noteworthy milestone in an individual's life, characterized by the emergence of fresh responsibilities, opportunities, and challenges. Various factors must be taken into account, such as education, employment, housing, healthcare, financial management, and social integration. These factors significantly influence the future path and overall well-being of individuals as they transition into adulthood.

Education plays a crucial role in equipping individuals for

adulthood and fostering independence. It is crucial for individuals with autism to have access to high-quality education that caters to their specific learning requirements and equips them for future achievements. Individuals in need may receive specialized services and supports, such as individualized education plans (IEPs), accommodations, and therapies that are specifically designed to address their strengths and challenges. In addition, promoting self-advocacy skills and encouraging autonomy in educational decision-making allows individuals to actively engage in shaping their educational experiences and preparing for their future goals.

Transition planning is an essential aspect of preparing for adulthood and independence. Transition planning is a process that entails working together to identify goals, explore opportunities, and develop strategies to support individuals as they make the transition from school to adult life. One possible approach is to consider various postsecondary education options, vocational training programs, employment opportunities, and independent living arrangements. It is crucial to initiate transition planning at an early stage and include key stakeholders such as parents, educators, healthcare providers, and community resources. This approach guarantees a well-coordinated and comprehensive support system for individuals to achieve their post-school aspirations.

Being well-prepared for employment is crucial when transitioning into adulthood and striving for independence. Obtaining meaningful and lucrative employment not only ensures financial stability but also promotes a sense of purpose, fulfillment, and social connectedness. Autistic individuals may benefit from targeted supports and accommodations to access employment opportunities that align with their interests, strengths, and abilities. These may include job coaching, assistive technology, and workplace accommodations. In addition, the promotion of inclusive hiring practices and the cultivation of supportive work environments that prioritize neurodiversity can pave the way for employment success and independence.

When preparing for adulthood and independence, it is important to carefully consider housing options. Individuals on the autism spectrum may have distinct housing preferences and support requirements that are influenced by their sensory sensitivities, social preferences, and level of independence. By considering various housing options, such as independent living, supported living arrangements, group homes, and transitional housing programs, individuals can discover housing solutions that align with their needs and preferences, promoting autonomy and independence.

Ensuring access to healthcare and developing self-management skills are crucial for individuals as they transition into adulthood and strive for independence. Individuals with autism may benefit from continuous healthcare support to effectively address their physical and mental health needs. It is important to have access to the right healthcare providers, a clear understanding of healthcare rights and responsibilities, and the ability to develop self-advocacy skills in order to navigate the healthcare system independently. In addition, the promotion of healthy lifestyle behaviors, such as proper nutrition, regular exercise, and effective stress management, plays a significant role in enhancing overall well-being and fostering independence.

Having a strong understanding of financial literacy and management skills is essential when it comes to preparing for adulthood and achieving independence. It can be advantageous for individuals with autism to acquire practical skills in budgeting, banking, saving, and independently managing their finances. It is crucial to have a comprehensive grasp of financial concepts, including income, expenses, taxes, and investments. Additionally, it is important to be aware of the available resources and support services that can aid in the development of financial independence and security for the future.

Ensuring social integration and community participation are crucial elements in the preparation for adulthood and independence. Developing social connections, nurturing friendships, and engaging in community activities and organizations are essential for fostering a sense of belonging, receiving social support, and enhancing overall well-being. Targeted social skills training, peer support groups, and community-based programs can be valuable for individuals with autism. These interventions aim to improve social interaction, communication, and relationship-building skills, ultimately helping them navigate social situations and establish meaningful connections with others.

Having a strong foundation in legal and advocacy skills is crucial when it comes to preparing for adulthood and independence. It is important for individuals with autism to have a clear understanding of their legal rights and responsibilities. This includes being aware of matters such as guardianship, healthcare decision-making, housing rights, employment rights, and disability accommodations. Enhancing one's ability to advocate for themselves and others involves developing self-advocacy skills and utilizing available resources and support services. This enables individuals to assert their rights, navigate complex systems, and effectively advocate for their needs.

Recognizing and embracing one's cultural and personal identity is crucial in the process of transitioning into adulthood and gaining independence. Autistic individuals, similar to all individuals, possess a wide range of cultural backgrounds, identities, and experiences that influence their understanding of themselves and sense of belonging. Embracing diversity, cultivating cultural understanding, and creating inclusive spaces that value and acknowledge individual identities are essential for fostering a strong sense of pride, belonging, and self-acceptance. These factors play a crucial role in empowering individuals to navigate the challenges of transitioning to adulthood with confidence and resilience.

Preparing for adulthood and independence is a complex process that necessitates meticulous planning, effective collaboration, and comprehensive support from a range of stakeholders. By addressing important areas such as education, transition planning, employment readiness, housing options, healthcare access, financial literacy, social integration, legal advocacy, and cultural affirmation, individuals can successfully navigate the transition to adulthood with confidence, autonomy, and resilience. By implementing proactive planning, providing targeted supports, and embracing inclusive practices, individuals on the autism spectrum can reach their maximum potential and experience fulfilling, self-determined lives as engaged members of their communities.

Long-Term Resilience And Success

Future planning requires a focus on long-term resilience and success, especially for individuals, including those on the autism spectrum, as they transition into adulthood and beyond. This topic explores the strategies, mindset, and resources required to develop resilience and attain long-term success throughout one's life. This concept covers a wide range of factors, such as personal growth, setting objectives, being adaptable, advocating for oneself, receiving support from the community, and continuous learning. All of these elements contribute to building resilience and achieving long-term success.

An essential factor for achieving long-term resilience and success is the development of a growth mindset. A growth mindset is defined by a belief in one's capacity to acquire knowledge, develop, and adjust to obstacles over a period of time. People who possess a growth mindset perceive setbacks and failures as chances for learning and personal development rather than as permanent obstacles. By cultivating a growth mindset, individuals are able to approach challenges in life with a positive outlook, resilience, and a determination to overcome obstacles.

Setting goals is an essential element for achieving long-term resilience and success. Establishing precise and attainable objectives offers individuals guidance, inspiration, and a sense of meaning. Having a clear plan for the future is essential for individuals to remain focused, organized, and proactive in pursuing their academic, career, personal, or social goals. In addition, by breaking larger goals into smaller, more manageable steps, individuals can effectively track their progress and celebrate achievements. This approach fosters a sense of accomplishment and momentum.

Flexibility is crucial when it comes to navigating the intricacies of life and attaining lasting success. Adapting to unforeseen circumstances is essential for building resilience in the face of life's unpredictable challenges. Autistic individuals, similar to all individuals, may face unexpected challenges, transitions, and opportunities throughout their lives. Developing flexibility, problem-solving skills, and coping mechanisms enables individuals to effectively navigate change, overcome obstacles, and thrive in diverse environments.

Developing the ability to advocate for oneself is crucial for maintaining resilience and achieving long-term success. Autistic individuals, similar to all individuals, possess distinct needs, preferences, and strengths that may necessitate accommodation and support. Mastering the skill of effectively expressing one's needs, asserting one's rights, and seeking out resources and accommodations is crucial for individuals to advocate for themselves in different contexts such as education, employment, healthcare, and social settings. In addition, establishing a network of supportive allies and mentors who can offer guidance and assistance enhances one's capacity to advocate for oneself and effectively navigate various systems.

Community support is essential for fostering long-term resilience and success. Establishing a strong network of family, friends, mentors, and community resources is crucial for individuals to receive emotional validation, practical assistance, and social connections, all of which are vital for their well-being and overall success. Autistic individuals can find value in accessing support groups, advocacy organizations, and community-based programs that offer specialized resources, peer support, and opportunities for social engagement and skill-building.

Continual learning and skill development are crucial for sustaining long-term resilience and achieving success. Continual learning supports a sense of intellectual curiosity, personal growth, and professional advancement, allowing individuals to adjust to shifting circumstances, explore new areas of interest, and remain current in a constantly changing world. Autistic individuals can derive significant advantages from participating in educational and vocational training programs, as well as continuing education opportunities. These initiatives provide them with the necessary resources to develop their skills, align with their interests, and work towards achieving their career goals.

Prioritizing wellness and self-care is crucial for maintaining long-term resilience and achieving success. Placing importance on physical, emotional, and mental well-being enables individuals to uphold equilibrium, cope with stress, and sustain optimal levels of performance in the long run. Implementing mindfulness practices, sensory regulation techniques, and self-soothing strategies into the daily routines of individuals with autism can be advantageous in fostering relaxation, self-awareness, and emotional regulation. In addition, cultivating a balanced lifestyle that incorporates consistent physical activity, wholesome nutrition, sufficient rest, and meaningful social interactions promotes general well-being and fortitude.

Effective financial planning and management play a crucial role in ensuring long-term resilience and success. Developing financial literacy skills, setting financial goals, and implementing sound money management practices are beneficial for autistic individuals, just like for all individuals. This encompasses budgeting, saving, investing, and planning for long-term financial security. By establishing a solid financial base and making well-informed choices regarding finances, individuals can attain enhanced stability, autonomy, and the ability to pursue their ambitions and aspirations.

Achieving long-term resilience and success involves a range of factors and is a constantly evolving process. It requires careful planning, continuous learning, the ability to adapt, and the support of the community. Individuals can develop resilience and skills to thrive throughout their lives by fostering a growth mindset, setting goals, cultivating adaptability, advocating for themselves, accessing community support, prioritizing wellness, continuing to learn and grow, and managing finances wisely. By dedicating themselves to personal growth and actively pursuing development, individuals on the autism spectrum can unlock their complete potential and experience gratifying, self-directed lives as valued contributors to their communities.

CONCLUSION

EMBRACING THE JOURNEY

Celebrating Progress and Growth

Recognizing and acknowledging progress and growth is a crucial element in embracing the journey, particularly for individuals on the autism spectrum and their families. This approach highlights the significance of acknowledging and valuing the small achievements, gradual enhancements, and notable milestones that occur during the journey of personal growth and learning. By emphasizing progress instead of striving for perfection, an environment is created that fosters self-esteem, motivation, and resilience.

To comprehend progress in the context of autism, it is important to recognize the distinct developmental paths and varied manifestations of growth. Autistic individuals may demonstrate non-linear patterns of growth, with skills and abilities emerging in bursts or in seemingly unpredictable ways, in contrast to the more linear and predictable progressions often observed in neurotypical development. Recognizing and appreciating unique patterns is essential to celebrating progress. It is important to value each step forward, regardless of its size, as a significant achievement.

An important factor in acknowledging progress and development is cultivating a mindset that appreciates hard work and perseverance. This mindset, commonly known as a growth mindset, promotes the idea of perceiving challenges as chances for learning and personal growth. When individuals, such as parents, caregivers, educators, and peers, embrace a growth mindset, they have the ability to demonstrate and reinforce the notion that putting in effort results in progress and development. This can be especially beneficial for individuals on the autism spectrum, who may encounter distinct difficulties and barriers. By acknowledging and valuing the dedication and determination of individuals, we contribute to the development of a strong and enduring framework that fosters sustained progress and achievement.

Concrete examples demonstrate the effectiveness of acknowledging and fostering progress and development. Consider, for example, a young child with autism who faces challenges in verbal communication. With the assistance of speech therapy and regular practice, the child gradually develops the ability to communicate basic needs using a limited vocabulary. This accomplishment, although it may appear insignificant to certain individuals, represents a significant advancement for the child and their family. Recognizing and acknowledging this progress serves to validate the child's hard work and fosters ongoing growth. Furthermore, it emphasizes the significance of exhibiting patience and perseverance, showcasing how progress is frequently achieved through continuous dedication and assistance.

In the educational setting, it is not uncommon for autistic students to face challenges when it comes to participating in group activities or completing assignments on their own. By providing personalized assistance, offering encouragement, and gradually introducing the student to social and academic difficulties, they start to engage more actively in class and accomplish tasks with growing self-reliance. Every stage of this journey, starting from initial cautious engagement to developing a more assured presence, signifies notable advancement. Recognizing these significant achievements acknowledges the diligent effort and unwavering commitment of the student, cultivating a strong sense of fulfillment and personal value.

Recognizing progress and growth goes beyond acknowledging individual achievements. It also involves appreciating the collective efforts of families, educators, therapists, and communities. Supporting an individual with autism requires a collaborative approach, with the contributions of many individuals playing a crucial role in the individual's development. Recognizing and appreciating these combined efforts emphasizes the importance of collaboration and mutual accountability. Furthermore, fostering a sense of community and connectedness is crucial for creating a supportive environment.

It is crucial to uphold practical and personalized expectations when acknowledging achievements. Every person with autism has their own distinct set of strengths, challenges, and rate of progress. It is important to establish goals that are achievable and significant for the individual, rather than measuring them against neurotypical peers or arbitrary benchmarks. Our approach centers around individualized objectives and acknowledging the successful attainment of these objectives. This fosters a constructive and nurturing environment that promotes ongoing progress and advancement.

Recognizing that setbacks and challenges are inherent to the process is an important aspect of embracing the journey. Progress often follows a non-linear path, with occasional challenges and setbacks. Recognizing progress entails acknowledging the determination and bravery needed to overcome obstacles and persevere. By presenting challenges as valuable learning experiences, we can assist individuals with autism in cultivating coping mechanisms and resilience, enabling them to surmount barriers and attain enduring success.

In addition, acknowledging progress and development requires providing chances for contemplation and recognition. It is important to dedicate time for introspection and contemplate past accomplishments and the progress made so far. This practice can offer valuable insights and help gain a broader perspective. It enables individuals and their supporters to acknowledge their progress, value the effort and perseverance required, and establish fresh objectives for the future. Reflection can also assist in identifying strategies and approaches that have proven to be highly effective, offering a clear path for ongoing growth and development.

Active participation from the community is crucial in acknowledging and commemorating advancements and developments. Creating inclusive communities that value and support diversity is crucial for fostering environments where autistic individuals can thrive. Communities play a crucial role in creating opportunities for autistic individuals to showcase their strengths and achievements by promoting awareness, understanding, and acceptance. Events like autism awareness campaigns, talent shows, and community gatherings serve as platforms to acknowledge and celebrate the valuable contributions and achievements of individuals with autism. These events serve the purpose of celebrating progress and promoting a sense of belonging and inclusion.

Recognizing and acknowledging the advancements and developments is a crucial aspect of embracing the path for individuals on the autism spectrum and those who support them. By acknowledging and appreciating the distinct developmental paths and gradual accomplishments of individuals with autism, we establish an atmosphere that fosters self-worth, drive, and adaptability. Creating an environment that promotes continuous growth and development involves fostering a growth mindset, setting realistic and individualized expectations, recognizing collective efforts, and providing opportunities for reflection and community involvement. These factors collectively contribute to a positive and supportive atmosphere. By implementing these strategies, we can assist individuals with autism in reaching their maximum potential and living meaningful, self-directed lives.

Continuing the Path to Resilience

The pursuit of resilience is a continuous endeavor, especially for individuals on the autism spectrum and their families. Embracing this journey involves acknowledging that resilience is not a static characteristic but rather a fluid process that develops and changes over time. It encompasses ongoing expansion, adjustment, and the formulation of strategies to navigate the obstacles and uncertainties of life. To fully comprehend and foster resilience, it is essential to adopt a comprehensive approach that addresses the emotional, social, and practical dimensions of life.

Resilience in the context of autism extends beyond mere problem-solving; it entails flourishing despite challenges and constructing a gratifying, self-directed existence. It is important to recognize that every individual on the autism spectrum has their own distinct set of strengths, challenges, and ways of engaging with the world. It is essential to cater to these specific needs in order to promote resilience. Our personalized approach fosters an environment that enables individuals with autism to unlock their potential and cultivate the self-assurance needed to confront challenges directly.

An essential aspect of furthering the journey towards resilience involves nurturing emotional resilience. Emotional resilience encompasses the capacity to comprehend and regulate one's emotions, uphold a positive perspective, and bounce back from adversity. Developing emotional resilience can pose a unique challenge for individuals on the autism spectrum, given the variations in emotional regulation and sensory processing. Nevertheless, with appropriate assistance and effective tactics, this goal can be fully realized. Various techniques, including mindfulness, cognitive-behavioral therapy, and sensory integration, have been found to be beneficial. These strategies assist individuals in identifying their emotions, comprehending their triggers, and cultivating coping mechanisms to effectively navigate emotional challenges.

Social support plays a crucial role in the development and sustenance of resilience. A robust support network offers individuals a feeling of inclusion, affirmation, and tangible aid. Autistic individuals can receive social support from a range of sources, such as family members, friends, educators, therapists, and peer groups. It is crucial to establish inclusive environments that foster acceptance and value for individuals on the autism spectrum. This inclusion promotes social connections and offers opportunities for individuals with autism to cultivate interpersonal skills and relationships that are essential for building resilience.

Academic and professional accomplishments are crucial aspects of the journey towards resilience. Education is crucial in providing autistic individuals with the necessary knowledge and skills for their success. Customized educational methods that cater to the unique learning styles and individual needs of students with autism can greatly contribute to their academic and personal development. In order to promote independence and self-sufficiency, it is essential to provide vocational training and employment opportunities. Employers can contribute to the career development and long-term success of autistic individuals by creating work environments that are supportive and accommodating.

In addition, promoting resilience requires promoting a proactive approach to problem-solving and decision-making. It is important to empower individuals with autism to actively participate in their lives, make well-informed decisions, and advocate for their needs. It is crucial for individuals to possess self-advocacy skills, as they allow them to clearly express their preferences, actively pursue necessary accommodations, and assert their rights. By introducing these skills early on and offering ample opportunities for practice, individuals on the autism spectrum can develop increased confidence and resilience in multiple areas of their lives.

In order to further enhance resilience, it is crucial to also focus on the development of practical life skills. Developing proficiency in daily living skills, including time management, financial literacy, and self-care, is crucial for fostering independence and self-efficacy. These skills can be acquired through direct instruction, modeling, and practice. Offering opportunities for individuals with autism to acquire and proficiently apply these skills in practical situations strengthens their capacity to effectively navigate their lives and boosts their overall adaptability.

An important aspect of resilience involves the capacity to adjust to changes and successfully navigate through transitions. Life is filled with various transitions, such as the shift from education to employment, adjustments in living arrangements, and acclimating to unfamiliar social settings.

Transitions can pose a significant challenge for individuals with autism due to their strong preference for routine and predictability. Nevertheless, with adequate preparation and the necessary support, individuals can effectively navigate these changes. Transition planning should incorporate a methodical approach to introducing individuals to unfamiliar settings, ensuring effective and unambiguous communication, and actively engaging supportive networks. Through careful preparation and providing a structured and supportive environment, individuals on the autism spectrum can develop the necessary adaptability and confidence to successfully navigate transitions and excel in unfamiliar circumstances.

Ensuring physical well-being is crucial for building resilience. The state of one's physical health significantly influences their emotional and mental well-being. It is crucial to promote a healthy lifestyle that encompasses regular exercise, balanced nutrition, and sufficient rest. In order to ensure overall well-being, it is crucial to address any co-occurring health issues, such as anxiety, depression, or sleep disorders. Having access to healthcare professionals who have a deep understanding of the specific needs of individuals with autism can greatly impact the effective management of these conditions.

Family support is crucial for maintaining resilience. Autistic individuals often rely on their families as their main source of support, receiving emotional, practical, and financial assistance from them. Providing families with education, resources, and respite care can assist them in their caregiving responsibilities and promote their own resilience. Family support groups and counseling are beneficial for individuals seeking a platform to share their experiences, gain valuable insights, and receive emotional support.

Community engagement is a crucial element of resilience. Being a member of a community that places importance on diversity and inclusion is crucial to fostering a sense of connection and support for individuals on the autism spectrum. Community programs, recreational activities, and volunteer opportunities offer valuable opportunities for individuals to engage in social interaction, develop new skills, and experience personal growth. These experiences contribute to a strong sense of belonging and purpose, which are crucial for building resilience.

In order to maintain resilience, it is crucial to remain dedicated to continuous learning and personal development throughout one's life. The journey continues beyond childhood and adolescence, extending into adulthood and beyond. It is highly recommended that individuals on the autism spectrum are supported in their pursuit of their interests, exploration of new opportunities, and ongoing development of their skills. There are various ways to engage in lifelong learning, such as pursuing formal education, vocational training, engaging in hobbies, and participating in personal development activities. Through adopting a mindset of ongoing improvement and curiosity, individuals on the autism spectrum can further enhance their resilience and reach their maximum potential.

In conclusion, the journey towards resilience is a complex and continuous endeavor that necessitates a comprehensive approach. Emotional resilience, social support, education, vocational opportunities, practical life skills, adaptability, physical health, family support, community engagement, and lifelong learning are all essential elements that contribute significantly to overall well-being. Through the careful cultivation of these elements and the provision of customized assistance, we can assist individuals on the autism spectrum in developing and sustaining the fortitude required to effectively navigate the obstacles of life and attain enduring accomplishments. Embracing the journey of resilience involves acknowledging achievements, gaining insights from challenges, and persistently pursuing personal development and satisfaction.

www.ingramcontent.com/pod-product-compliance
Lightning Source LLC
Chambersburg PA
CBHW061344160726
47995CB00001B/172